Seven Steps to the Marriage Altar

How to Practice the Prinicples of Betrothal

by
Douglas Hammett

Seven Steps to the Marriage Altar:
How to Practice the Principles of Betrothal

by
Douglas Hammett

ISBN# 978-0-86645-285-4

All Scripture quotations taken from King James Version

The picture on the cover is of our daughter and son-in-law at the
time of their betrothal.

Printed by:

Challenge Press
4702 Colebrook Avenue
Emmaus, PA 18049
www.lvbaptist.org

Table of Contents

Chapter One
Introduction

Of all the love stories in the Bible, I think there are none that are any more beautiful than the story of Ruth and Boaz. It is one that my heart thrills at every time I think about it and read it or preach on it. We want to specifically look at how Ruth gets to the marriage altar, found in chapter 3.

"Then Naomi her mother in law said unto her, My daughter, shall I not seek rest for thee, that it may be well with thee?

And now is not Boaz of our kindred, with whose maidens thou wast? Behold, he winnoweth barley to night in the threshingfloor.

Wash thyself therefore, and anoint thee, and put thy raiment upon thee, and get thee down to the floor: but make not thyself known unto the man, until he shall have done eating and drinking.

And it shall be, when he lieth down, that thou shalt mark the place where he shall lie, and thou shalt go in, and uncover his feet, and lay thee down; and he will tell thee what thou shalt do.

And she said unto her, All that thou sayest unto me I will do.

And she went down unto the floor, and did according to all that her mother in law bade her.

And when Boaz had eaten and drunk, and his heart was merry, he went to lie down at the end of the heap of corn: and she came softly, and uncovered his feet, and laid her down.

And it came to pass at midnight, that the man was afraid, and turned himself: and, behold, a woman lay at his feet.

And he said, Who art thou? And she answered, I am Ruth thine handmaid: spread therefore thy skirt over thine handmaid; for thou art a near kinsman.

And he said, Blessed be thou of the LORD, my daughter: for thou hast shewed more kindness in the latter end than at the beginning, inasmuch as thou followedst not young men, whether poor or rich.

And now, my daughter, fear not; I will do to thee all that thou requirest: for all the city of my people doth know that thou art a virtuous woman." (Ruth 3:1-11)

I am not going to be able to cover the whole story of Ruth in detail, but I want to hit the highlights for you. In chapter one Naomi returns to her homeland of Bethlehem-judah. She has come back with her daughter-in-law Ruth. Both of these ladies have been recently widowed.

Ruth, the daughter-in-law, was a Moabite woman, but she has left the country of her birth and her idolatry and believed in Jehovah-God of the Jews. Her life has been transformed and she has made a commitment to stay with her mother-in-law and care for her.

In the first verse of chapter 3 it is clear that Ruth has gone to "sleep" as far as her desire for a husband is concerned. She is not the one that is requesting the issue of a husband. Instead, it is Naomi that has her eyes on a certain man that she thinks will be a good match for Ruth.

In verse two, Naomi begins to talk about Boaz who is of their kindred. In Deuteronomy chapter 25, God had commanded that when a man and a woman were married and the man died without an heir having been born, then the next unmarried male of his kin was to marry the young lady. He was called a kinsman-redeemer. Usually the next of kin would be a brother. But in this case, there were no living brothers.

In verse three Naomi explains to Ruth what she is to do. She was to take a bath, put on clean clothes, and then present herself to Boaz at the threshingfloor where he was threshing wheat. Naomi gave her specific instructions on just how to do that.

In verse four Ruth agrees to do exactly what her mother-in-law has told her to do. So she goes to present herself to Boaz. When you read this story, you might have some questions about what exactly is going on. I won't go into all the details, but let me just say that this was a very public place, there were servants all around, and what she was doing was not improper in any way.

When Boaz wakes up at midnight and realizes that there is a woman at his feet, Ruth presents herself as the kin of Boaz, and reminds him of his responsibility. Boaz admits in verse eleven that not only is he willing to fulfill his responsibility, but he extols her virtue and calls her a virtuous woman.

I find it quite interesting that Boaz, a Jewish man, called Ruth, a Moabite woman, a virtuous woman. Ruth had been a pagan, and even though she had turned to the Lord, she would have still been considered a Gentile dog by most of the Jews. Yet, Boaz had seen her true character.

If you are familiar with your Bible, you know the end of the story. Ruth not only ends up marrying Boaz, but they become the great-grandparents of King David. Ultimately, she is listed in the lineage of the Lord Jesus Christ.

From Principles to Practice

How does a person get to the marriage altar in a godly way that is pleasing to God and does not violate the principles of scripture? That is the question we want to answer in this book.

God was the One who instituted marriage. He said, "It is not good for a man to be alone." Yet in our world today, mankind has perverted what God originally intended. Many marriages end in divorce. Others just decide to live together and not even get married. In the legislature they debate about the real definition of marriage.

But please don't despair. God still has the answer, if we will take time to find it in the Word of God. We want to look at how to get to a marriage relationship through God-ordained authority so that we are able to keep ourselves from making a very unwise choice in marriage.

My heart breaks as I see young people go out on their own and decide to do their own fishing, looking for a marriage partner. They disregard what God says, what their parents say, and what their pastor says.

So they date this one and that one, and another one. Finally they settle on a marriage partner, but they are blinded to their wrong choice. If you try to warn them about the danger ahead, they will get angry.

I have done much study on this subject over the years, and I have found basically three principles in the Word of God that relate to getting to the marriage altar. I am going to briefly lay out those three principles for you and then we are going to look at seven steps to getting to the marriage altar. (If you would like a more detailed look at these three principles, see the e-book, ***Dating, Courtship and Betrothal: Sorting out Marriage Matters with Bible Principles,*** available at this link: *http://www.purposedcoachingblog.com/about/ebooks-by-doug-hammett/dating-courtship-and-betrothal-sorting-out-marriage-matters-with-bible-principles/*)

A principle is a truth that God gives us in the Word of God. Our practice should then be carried out in such a way that it does not violate the principles of God's Word. The seven steps to getting to the marriage altar are practical truths or ways that you can go about implementing these three principles of marriage that are found in the Word of God.

Principle One—*Reserve romance for a committed relationship.* A committed relationship refers to a betrothal relationship that is going to end in marriage. That is the only place that romance belongs.

Principle Two—*A committed relationship is to be unconditional.* When the betrothal commitment is made, it is as guaranteed as marriage is meant to be. The marriage vows are until death do us part. A betrothal commitment says we are going to get married. It is not like an engagement which can be broken by either party. Before we enter into a commitment with someone, we need to be sure we are committed to go all the way.

Principle Three—*Enter the relationship only with parental protection and permission.* The parents of both the young man and the young lady need to be involved in the whole process.

It is the job of the father of the young lady to guard his daughter's purity and then to give her in marriage when the right young man comes along. The parents of the young man have the responsibility to teach and train the young man, to help him to stay asleep until he is ready for marriage, and then to guide him in the process of finding the young lady that God has for him to marry.

The Seven Steps

What are the seven steps for getting to marriage? We are going to walk through the seven steps first, and talk about them briefly. Then we will come back and cover each of them in more detail.

The first step is that of being *asleep*. When you are first born, you don't recognize that there is any difference between men and women. But as you get older, you begin to see that difference.

God's intent is that you not get stirred up in your heart towards the opposite sex until the time comes that you are ready for marriage. So this asleep period is a description of how our lives ought to be governed when we are in the single status. We need to be asleep as far as the stirring of the emotions towards the opposite sex.

During this time of single life, a person is to be concerned about living for Jesus Christ and serving Him with all their heart. You should guard your heart against getting all cluttered up with changing emotions or getting entangled with someone of the opposite sex. Your goal is to serve Christ.

The next step is that of being *alert*. The time comes when you wake up and realize that it is time to start moving towards marriage. You have learned how to manage your heart and to keep yourself from going astray with lustful desire motivating your life. You are now ready to consider marriage.

The next step is the *approach*. A young man finds the girl that he thinks is the right one for him to marry, and his parents think she is the right one also. We will look later at how to make that approach.

The next step is *assessment*. The young man and his parents need to make an assessment of the young lady to figure out if she is indeed the right one. The young lady and her parents need to make an assessment of the young man as well. This assessment needs to be done in a proper guarded manner. The purpose is to be Christ-focused first and then character focused second, so that these two young people will make a decision that is a Godly decision instead of a selfish decision made by emotions.

The next step is *agreement*. This is the betrothal stage. Both sets of parents and the young man and the young lady all agree that this is God's will. Now they have become a couple. They have determined that they are going all the way to the marriage altar. There is no physical involvement or contact during this period, but they are going to get to know each other.

The next step is the *attraction* step. During this betrothal period, their hearts are becoming entwined. They are building a connection in their hearts with one another, apart from physical involvement. Once the physical involvement begins—kissing, hugging, petting— they stop talking and they don't learn how to communicate.

During this step, the young man and the young lady will have the greatest desire to get to know one another. That is how God designed it. That is why it is so important to establish the heart connection and to learn good communication. They are building their affection for one another and building a security in the relationship.

The final step is the *altar.* Now they are husband and wife, and the physical contact begins. They can have their first kiss at the marriage altar. They have kept themselves clean and pure. Their marriage is meant to be the beginning of a great witness to the rest of the world.

In the following chapters we want to look at each of these steps in more detail. God has a proper way for us to get to the marriage altar. Are we concerned about doing things God's way?

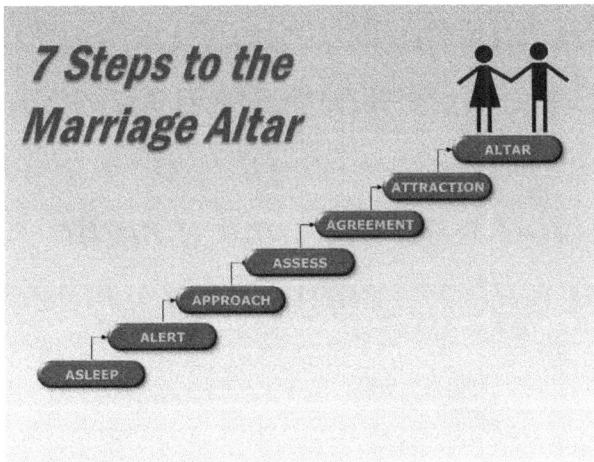

7 Steps to the Marriage Altar

In this step of being asleep,
you are waiting on God
and preparing your life so that when
God says the time it right,
you will be ready for marriage.

Chapter Two
First Step—Asleep

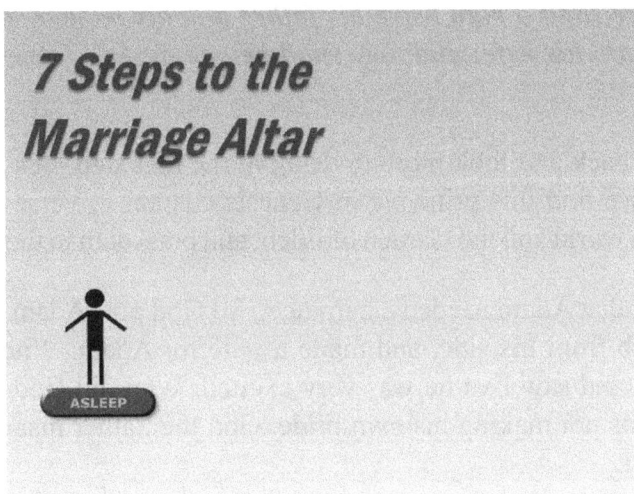

"And the LORD God said, It is not good that the man should be alone; I will make him an help meet for him.

And out of the ground the LORD God formed every beast of the field, and every fowl of the air; and brought them unto Adam to see what he would call them: and whatsoever Adam called every living creature, that was the name thereof.

And Adam gave names to all cattle, and to the fowl of the air, and to every beast of the field; but for Adam there was not found an help meet for him.

And the LORD God caused a deep sleep to fall upon Adam, and he slept: and he took one of his ribs, and closed up the flesh instead thereof;

And the rib, which the LORD God had taken from man, made he a woman, and brought her unto the man.

And Adam said, This is now bone of my bones, and flesh of my flesh: she shall be called Woman, because she was taken out of Man.

Therefore shall a man leave his father and his mother, and shall cleave unto his wife; and they shall be one flesh." (Genesis 2:18-24)

Let's go back and look more in detail at the first step, that of being asleep. We find this principle in Genesis chapter 2, verse 21. God made the world and the Garden of Eden, and put Adam in the Garden.

God saw that Adam needed a helpmeet. So God puts Adam to sleep, took a rib from his side, and made a wife for Adam. When Adam woke up and saw Eve he was very excited. Why did God do that? Adam was not making his own bride. God the Father made a bride for Adam.

I want to point out something in verse 24. When a man leaves his father and his mother, he is supposed to move to his wife and connect his heart to her. Today what we see happening is that while the young man is living at home with Mom and Dad, he plays the field, so to speak. He dates one girl and then another girl and then another girl.

What ends up happening in the young man and young lady's life is that they wind up giving pieces of their heart to first one person and then another and they end up with broken hearts. All the while their hearts are being alienated more and more from their father and their mother.

God's intent is that when they leave father and mother, they are to cleave to their wife. The two happenings are to be simultaneous. They are to take place together and under parental authority.

Three Stages of Life

There are three stages of life. You are either single, or betrothed, or married. If you are single, you don't have a wife. If you are betrothed, you have a wife-in-waiting. She is committed to you, you are committed to her, but you are not moved in together yet. Then there is the final stage, which is marriage. Those are the three stages of life that God has ordained.

Let me just mention here that engagement is not betrothal. They are very different, even though many people try to say that they are the same thing. Let me try to explain the difference briefly.

Engagement is often used as a trial period for the young man and the young lady to see if they can get along with each other. If they can't get along, then either party can break the engagement. I have known of people that have been involved in engagements over 6 times and not ended up getting married. God never intended that to be the case.

God intends that when betrothal takes place, it is a full commitment to go all the way to marriage. The young man and the young lady as well as the parents have all agreed to the marriage taking place. During the betrothal period, it is a time of building with one another a relationship that will lead into the final stage, which is marriage.

In this step of being asleep, you are waiting on God and preparing your life so that when God says the time it right, you will be ready for marriage. Many young people get in a hurry to get married. If they are still single by the time they turn 20, they began to get itchy and think life has passed them by. But the average age today for marriage is now 28. Young people, you need to relax—you have plenty of time.

During the entire single stage, the heart and the emotions of the young man and the young lady in regards to the opposite sex are to be asleep. Listen to the advice that God gave to Timothy through the Apostle Paul in First Timothy chapter five.

"Rebuke not an elder, but intreat him as a father; and the young men as brethren; The elder women as mothers; the younger as sisters, with all purity." (First Timothy 5:1-2)

Paul instructs young Timothy on the way that he is deal with the people in the church. The older men are to be approached as a father, the younger men are to be treated like a brother.

Teenagers, are you listening? You go to school here at our Christian school, and there are some younger guys that are there too. You don't belong treating them wrong just because you are bigger than they are. You ought to be looking out for them, treating them like they are a brother in Christ—which means you treat them with respect, love and concern.

The elder women are to be treated as mother. How would you treat your mother? That is the way you ought to treat every older woman in the church. Any lady that is older than you ought to be treated as if she were your mother.

Then the younger ladies are to be treated as sisters. In other words, the younger women in the church are to be treated as sisters in Christ. Then he adds these words—with all purity.

Guys, you don't belong putting your hands on the girls. You don't belong trying to get their attention and stirring their emotions. You don't belong standing between them and their parents. You are to treat them like they are a sister, and do it with all purity.

The only way you can do that and treat them like a sister is if you are asleep. In other words, you are not looking on them as someone of the opposite sex that you are attracted to. You are not trying to get their attention and hope they will be attracted to you.

If that is your attitude, you have not treated her like a sister. You have treated her like an object. There is a problem in your heart. That is what Paul is warning about.

When we talk about being asleep, we mean that you don't look on them with eyes of lust or with a desire to get something from them. You look on them as if they were your sister—you look on them appropriately. That is what it means to be asleep.

You might say, "That is not how I feel about certain young ladies that I happen to know." Then the problem is not with the young lady—the problem is with your heart. You need to put your heart back to sleep.

Purpose of Single Life

The very purpose of the single life is found in First Corinthians 7:32-33.

"But I would have you without carefulness. He that is unmarried careth for the things that belong to the Lord, how he may please the Lord. But he that is married careth for the things that are of the world, how he may please his wife."

Some people have read these verses in First Corinthians chapter seven and concluded that Paul is saying that it is wrong to get married. As a single person, is it wrong to desire to marry?

No, there is nothing wrong with that. It is not wrong to get married. In these verses, Paul is just warning that with marriage comes difficulty and problems.

Many times I have been sitting with a couple that want to get married, and I can tell they are going to have problems. But when I try to counsel them and warn them about the dangers and difficulties ahead, it falls on deaf ears. They are not listening, but they have already made up their minds.

Paul is saying that there is nothing wrong with getting married in the proper way and to the right person. But when you marry you are going to add to your life difficulties that you as a single person right now cannot even begin to imagine.

You might think it will not be that way, but let me tell you, it will be. You are a sinner, she is a sinner, and when you put two sinners together under the same roof, it doesn't add up to heaven.

To Please the Lord

So the goal and purpose of the single life is *to please the Lord*. A single young man or a single young lady ought to live caring for the Lord. Their lives ought to be centered on Christ. They ought to live to please Jesus. That is where their heart ought to be.

I can look back in my life and remember in those early years when I first got saved. God began to deal with my heart. I loved the Lord and wanted to please Him and serve Him and work for Him. My heart was entwined with His, and my desire was to serve Him with all that I had. I was all out for Christ.

Then a certain young lady came along and caught my attention. My attention was diverted from Christ to her. I was still in church and still serving the Lord, but all of a sudden there was division of attention.

Now there is a proper way to go about this process—and we will look at that as we get further along. You will still have some division of attention—that is necessary during the betrothal period and during marriage.

Any man that is married knows that is true. Your time is now divided as you have to care for your wife and your family. You have to provide for them and spend time with them if you are going to be a successful husband and father.

"There is a difference also between a wife and a virgin. The unmarried woman careth for the things of the Lord, that she may be holy both in body and in spirit: but she that is married careth for the things of the world, how she may please her husband." (First Corinthians 7:34)

Paul is not talking about the things of the world in a wrong sort of a way; he is not saying that she is worldly. But the world's interactions are going to claim her time.

Many women have complained to me over the years about how much time it takes to take care of the kids, wash the house, wash the clothes, fix the food, and they just don't have time to do other things in the spiritual realm.

Once they were single and they could serve at the church and be more involved. But marriage and family changes all of that.

That is exactly what Paul was talking about here. Anybody with any kind of insight looking forward could see this is true.

"And this I speak for your own profit; not that I may cast a snare upon you, but for that which is comely, and that ye may attend upon the Lord without distraction." (verse 35)

Paul wrote these words to help the believers—not to tell them they couldn't get married, but to warn them that this is what happens if you do get married.

Most people that are single, especially when they get up to about the age of twenty, think they will never get married. If you have that attitude, you will end up ruining the rest of the good years that you have left. If you are unhappy in being single, you will throw away the time you have to serve Jesus Christ.

In Philippians chapter four, Paul said that he had learned to be content in whatever state he was in. He was talking specifically about being in and out of prison, but it could just as well be applied to single vs. married and the state between the two. There is no reason that you cannot serve Christ with your life during this time of singleness.

To Prepare for Marriage

When a child is born, he/she is enrolled in marriage classes. It is an

18-24 year course of study, and there are many things that you learn over the years. These things all help to prepare you for your future marriage. Here are some of the things that you need to learn.

How does a husband treat his wife? How does a wife treat her husband? What is the right way to interact with one another? What should I expect when I get married?

How do I show respect? How do I handle disagreements? How do I show affection? How do I show submission and deference? How do I speak in a respectful way?

Those are just a few of the things that we learn as we are growing up and observing our parents. We don't necessarily stop and think about it when we are younger. Actually, we should be paying far more attention than what we do. But we are just taking it in while we are living in the family situation and we are learning how to treat our future spouse.

And I believe that is what this time period is—a course on how to treat your future husband or wife. We do learn by example, as First Corinthians 4:16 tells us. We become followers of others, and we do it without even realizing what we are doing.

Parents, you need to remember that your kids are watching you. Your sons and your daughters are watching how you treat each other as husband and wife, and how you express love and affection to each other. They are watching and they are learning.

Sir, do your children ever see you kiss and hug your wife? You don't have to be risqué or improper about it, but your wife ought to know you love her. And it needs to be done publicly enough that your kids know that you love her too.

Ladies, it ought to go the other way too, because the young ladies in your home are learning how to respond to their husbands when they get married. They are watching how you interact with your husband. There are men and women that never show affection to their spouse, and they end up training the next generation to have all kinds of marriage problems because of the lack of affection.

As we raise young men and young ladies, we need to recognize that they are to be raised differently. Boys and girls are different—they are different physically as well as functionally. They function different in the home.

There are also different responsibilities between young men and young ladies, different roles that they are being groomed to fill. They are different in how they dress—at least they ought to be different. They are to be different in their decision making processes.

Moms, I am not saying that you don't teach your young men how to wash dishes and how to cook. They need to know to know how to do those things, in case they never get married, so they can take care of themselves. But there are certain things around the house that I take care of—my wife doesn't have to take care of those.

Boys and girls are different in their deportment, in the way they handle themselves. They are to be different in the way that they interact with others. So the way that you raise them becomes very important.

Raising Girls

Let's look at some things that are specific with your daughters first. You need to teach your daughters *to defer decisions to their fathers.* This is a biblical practice.

First Corinthians 11:9 tells us that daughters are given in marriage. The Bible also says that the woman was created for the man. This has to do with order in the home.

The young lady is to learn how to give deferment to her father, so when she is married she can give deferment to her husband in decisions. It is God's order. She also needs to learn to balance that with a proper input of her observations and her understandings so that a proper decision can be made.

That means that as fathers, we need to learn how to listen and to weigh out what our daughters have to say, and make fair and right judgments for them. In this way they learn that they can interact with their husband.

Your daughter needs to be *trained to be a helpmeet*. They learn this by watching their mother. If Mom is a proper helpmeet who meets the needs of her husband, the young lady is going to learn by watching her mother. It will help her to be a fine wife in the future.

In Numbers chapter 30 the Bible says that a father has the responsibility to disavow a vow that his daughter makes when he hears of it. This is an important Bible principle.

There are times when a father needs to say, "I am sorry, this is not a good decision. We are not going to do this."

The daughter needs to be taught to take such issues to her father, and deferring the decision to him. The father then has the right of supporting the decision or disavowing the vow. This is preparing the young lady for the submission of Ephesians chapter five that will take place in the marriage relationship. Remember, you can never have two people who are both heads. It doesn't work well.

The father is also responsible for the virginity of his daughter (Deuteronomy 22:13-21). When your daughter comes to the marriage altar, you are responsible to make sure she comes there as a virgin. That means you need to know where she is at and what she is doing.

You need to protect her, care for her, and provide for her. It is your job as a father. She needs a protector, and you are her protector as long as she is unmarried. When she gets married, her husband assumes that role of protector.

Here are three areas worth giving some attention to with your daughters. First, *teach her how to deal with strangers.* Moms, you really need to be watchful in this area. Teach her how to be rude in a kind way, when strangers are too forward and say things to her that are inappropriate.

At the same time, you need to teach her how to have a gentle spirit, and the ability to say no in an appropriate way. Here is what I fear. I fear that in a lot of Bible-based families, people read about submission of the wife and they come away thinking that means the girl is supposed to just say yes, yes, yes to whoever and whatever.

That is not Bible. She needs to know how to have a backbone, how to stand up for what is right, how to speak her mind with confidence, and yet be able to defer to proper authority in her life when they need to make the decisions.

It is a blend that is very difficult to make happen, but it needs to be taught within the confines of the family before she ever gets married. If it is not, she may wind up marrying a guy that is overly pushy, and she will wind up in big trouble—all because Mom and Dad have not prepared her to handle that kind of an affront.

Second, she needs to know *how to create distance in casual relationships.* Young ladies that are overly flirtatious and always trying to get attention have not been given the proper training at home. Mom and Dad neglected to teach them that.

Young ladies need to know how to have a casual relationship with young men in the church and be able to talk with them. If she senses that there is anything that begins to heat up with either her or with a young man, she ought to step immediately out of the situation. Parents, you have the responsibility to teach her how to handle all of that.

Third, teach her *what to do when men approach her openly and honorably.* This is a right approach—and she needs to know how to handle that, how to defer it to her father, and how to speak in that particular matter.

Raising Boys

Let's look at the son now. Sons need to be taught something that is not taught in America today which is *Biblical masculinity.* We are in an effeminate culture in our world. Men are not men anymore—they have been effeminized. They are trying to get in touch with their feeling side so much, they have not been able to learn and stand and do what is right.

Dads, you need to interact with your sons, especially starting around eleven to twelve years of age. You need to get involved in their lives and teach them to be men. Don't leave them on their own to develop based on what the rest of their peers tells them they should be doing. You need to be teaching them.

Young men need to be taught *how to be independent,* so when they get married they are prepared to leave father and mother and cleave to their wife (Genesis 2:24). Ladies, as your son grows up, you are going to notice that around the ages of twelve or so, he will start to get a little sassy with you at home. It is not unusual.

Let me tell you why that happens. Inside, he is thinking, "I am a man. I am supposed to be in charge like dad is in charge." Mom, I don't recommend that you have to be the one to stop that. You need to stand up to them and let them know they are not acting appropriately.

But then you need to talk with your husband and let him take him down about five notches. Dads, it is your job. Your boys don't have any business treating your wife with any disrespect. You are teaching those young men how to properly relate to a lady.

You are also teaching them how to respond to authority, even though they think that they are bigger than the authority. Now, let me warn you. You need to do it when they are young.

If you wait until they are bigger, you might not be able to handle them. If you teach them when they are young how to treat their mother right, it will go much smoother in the home, especially as they get older.

On the other hand, you need to be careful that you don't break them of their desire for independence. That desire for independence is something that they are reared for, because they are eventually going to have to take charge in their own home. You want them to grow up able to make decisions and able to handle themselves.

You want them to be confident about making right decisions, able to move forward, able to have a backbone in their own life and stand up for what is right.

You don't want to turn them into some kind of a milk toast. But at the same time, you want to teach them how to treat ladies rightly.

Here are three important things to teach them. First, *teach him how to take initiative in relationships.* Teach him how to be able to talk with someone else. Teach him how to stand his own ground, and how to do it in such a way that he does not get intimidated and fearful just because someone is bigger than him.

There is also a flip side to this, and that is not to get a cocky, bull-headed attitude like you can be a bully and push other people over. It is a balancing act that men need to teach their boys so that they can stand up for what is right, and at the same time learn to be willing to sit down and lose their rights for the good of another person.

One of the best lessons I ever learned was when I was in junior high. Another boy in our school was always out for a fight and always picking a fight with someone. He was a bully's bully and I was scared to death of him.

One day he found out that I was in school. I don't know how he first noticed me, but he came and he singled me out. I had watched him start shoving on other guys and challenging them to a fight. He had most of them intimidated. I knew that if I went out and fought this boy, I was going to get killed. He was so much bigger than I was.

Then the day came when he came up and started shoving on me. I was backing and backing and backing, and I finally got enough and shoved him back. He got angry with me and said, "That's it. I will meet you outside after school at 4:00."

I said, "I'll be there," and then I started thinking, "What have I done?" Well, I did show up, but he didn't. Now, I don't know why he didn't show up, but I figured that the next day he would come after me again.

But the next day at school, he walked right by me in the halls like he didn't see me—and I didn't stop him. I learned an important lesson. There is a place for a man to stand up and stand his ground.

If you die standing, it is better than being pushed over and destroyed—if it is a matter worth fighting over. Some things aren't worth fighting over, and you are better off to back away and forget it. But a man needs to know how to stand and when to stand.

Second, you need to teach him *how to assess and assume risks.* He needs to know how to make decisions and how to calculate the risks. How much he is willing to risk? Is it really going to pay off, and is it worth the loss at the end?

A young man needs to be taught how to do that, because eventually he is going to scope out and find a young lady that he thinks might be the right one. He has to approach the father of the girl and there is a good possibility that the dad may say no.

That is hurtful to a young man. No man wants that to happen to them, but he needs to be willing to take that kind of a risk.

If he doesn't have enough backbone to step up and ask, and if he is not willing to take the risk of being turned down, then he doesn't belong with that young lady anyway. He is not worthy of her.

On the other hand, he needs to learn how to be able to take those risks and swallow his pride if he loses. He is asking that young lady to disrupt her whole life plans for his life so he needs to be willing to risk some of his pride for that young lady.

Third, you need to *teach him how to protect his moral life.* In Proverbs chapter five we find a father giving instruction to his son about how to handle a strange or a wicked woman. Fellows, you need to be the ones that teach your sons how to keep their heart and how to keep themselves from lust in this world.

Our world is full of lust and sexual sin. You can't drive down the street or turn on the radio or TV or internet without being assaulted by this trash everywhere.

Parents, I strongly recommend that you assess wisely your son's character before you ever let him go out into the world to get a job. It is a jungle out there, and you better have taught him how to handle himself and how to stand up to that kind of temptation.

How to Stay Asleep

So the question comes down to this—how do I stay asleep if I am a young man? Well, it boils down to a few things. First of all, you need to *avoid lust at all costs.* If you sit around and look at trash, you are going to wind up with lust in your heart. It will cause you trouble.

Second, *enlist your parent's help.* Our world today feeds the sensual lusts and cravings. If you want something that will destroy your marriage or greatly hurt your marriage, this will do it in a moment of time.

Young men, there are lots of older men in your life that could give you testimony as to how pornography, things on the internet, and illicit affairs have destroyed or greatly hurt their relationships with their wives. It is costly.

You may think that you can dabble in it and you can control it. But it is impossible to do. Many could share with you how their lives were greatly hurt by that kind of trash. It is not a wise thing to be involved in.

Once you start stirring up those emotions and those passions, they begin to take on a life of their own. Soon there is an inability to say no to them, and they will destroy you. Fathers, you and I need to pay attention to that in the lives of our sons.

God says that we are to mortify or put to death those ungodly lusts when they come into our hearts. Moral impropriety in the heart and lustful thoughts need to be stabbed and killed.

How can you do that practically as a young man? You can walk into your dad and say, "Dad, I need to tell you about something wrong in my heart right now and I need help."

Don't go to him unless you are ashamed and serious about getting rid of it. You will be stabbing it. You will be facing it. If you sit down with your dad and tell him what you are facing, he can help you to overcome that problem.

Second thing you need to do, you need to starve it. Dad, this is your responsibility to help him with that. It doesn't just happen overnight, but over a period of time.

How do you starve it? Cut him off from the influences that stir the heart in a wrong manner. You will need to figure out what those influences are in your son's life, and you will need to help him build those walls of protection in his life, so he can keep himself from falling into sin.

How long do you stay asleep? This is a stage of life that you need to stay in until God and your parents say your life is ready and prepared. Then you are ready to start thinking about marriage. Until that time, stay asleep!

Chapter Three
Step Two—Alert

We looked in the last chapter at the first step to the marriage altar, which is the step of being asleep. This is speaking of the time period in the early part of life before you are ready for marriage.

Some people are amazed that I teach on the subject of betrothal. I think the thing that amazes people the most is when I say that a young man and a young lady should not kiss until they get to the marriage altar. How can I say such a thing, especially in a society like ours today?

But it is real simple—I read First Corinthians 7:1 and I dared to believe what God says. *"It is good for a man not to touch a woman."* If you don't like that, don't argue with me—your argument is with God.

God knows what He is talking about, and He is not trying to make your life hard or keep something from you. He knows you need some guidance in order to get to your end destination with the least damage possible. So He set some practical guidelines for you to follow.

If you want to get married the world's way and get involved in the boyfriend/girlfriend scene, be ready for your life to get messed up. You will have a lot of heartache and heartbreak along the way. If you do it God's way, you will have a lot better chance that your marriage will turn out the way that God intended.

Now we want to move on to the next step, step two, which is the step of being alert. This is when a young man or young lady starts to notice those of the opposite sex. They are at a point in their life where they are ready for marriage, and they can start thinking about marriage.

Possess Your Vessel in Sanctification

When you get to this step, the direction and focus of your life ought to be that you are open to the leadership of the Lord. You attitude should be, "Not what I want, but what God wants for my life. I need to *find* the right kind of a person, but I need to also *be* the right kind of a person."

Parents, you will know when your young person gets to this the step of being alert, because all of a sudden they start thinking about the guys and the girls. They have been focusing in their single life on serving the Lord. But now they realize that God may have someone for them to marry and to spend the rest of their life with.

What happens if they start thinking about the opposite sex too early in their life? What if they wake up too soon? We talked in the first chapter about how to go back to sleep. If they are not ready for marriage, it is too early. They need to go back to sleep.

Just ask them, "Are you ready to get married?" They may think they are ready for a relationship with the opposite sex, but that is now what you are asking them.

If they are not ready to get married and handle all the responsibilities that go with that, they need to go back to sleep. A lot of young guys think they are ready for a romantic relationship, but that kind of a relationship is reserved for marriage.

"For this is the will of God, even your sanctification, that ye should abstain from fornication:

That every one of you should know how to possess his vessel in sanctification and honour:

Not in the lust of concupiscence, even as the Gentiles which know not God. (First Thessalonians 4:3-5)

This is what God wants in your life—He wants you set apart to serve Christ. You will never go wrong advising a young person to live a sanctified life. To be sanctified is to be set apart for the purpose of serving God—set apart from sin and set apart to serve Christ.

You will never go wrong in telling a young person to get their hands off the opposite sex. You will never go wrong in telling them to get their mind off of dwelling on the romance of the opposite sex when they are not married. God's will for everybody is that they are to be sanctified.

Paul said that we as Christians are to abstain from fornication. One of the ways that you destroy the sanctification and usefulness in your life is in the area of fornication. Fornication is any manner of sexual sin—physical or mental. It can even be the thought of the heart.

I know in our world it is a socially accepted thing for boys and girls to be in a relationship with each other. They are allowed to go off by themselves and do things they shouldn't do. Parents say, "That's just what kids do, and as long as she doesn't get pregnant, it is no big deal. Everything will be OK."

No, I am sorry, everything will not be OK. The moment their mind gets involved in it and they begin to lust in their heart, as far as God is concerned, they have committed adultery in their heart. When we are talking about the alert issue, one of the most important things involved is being sure you keep yourself right before God.

To possess your own vessel refers to two things. First, it is talking about my own body that I live in. I need to control and properly handle my own vessel—my own body. I need to have it in control at all times so it can be used in sanctification and honor for the Lord.

But according to First Peter, this passage also refers to possessing your future wife, the young lady that God has prepared for you to marry. There is a proper way to possess her, a proper way to get her as your wife—this involves how to approach her and how to acquire her. All of that is wrapped up in the issue of doing it in sanctification and in honor.

Young man, you don't belong going out there and saying, "Let's see how many girls I can spend time with and then I can pick the one that I want." Why is that wrong? First of all, you are in fornication. That is not how a child of God acts. So we have to even wonder whether or not you are a child of God.

The second problem is that you have now spent time with and taken liberties with those young ladies who will someday be married to someone else. You have messed them up and the rest of their life they will remember that relationship with you.

How will that affect and infect their relationship with their future husband? How will it cause them to withdraw and not want to give themselves in love to their own husband? How will it cause them to put up bars and walls in order to protect themselves?

When we talk about alertness, we are talking about possessing our own body right, and then possessing the vessel of the young lady we are going to marry in sanctification and honor. We need to be sure that we approach the marriage altar in a right way. The wrong way is seen in verse five—in the lust of concupiscence. That is the way of the world.

Call to Prepare

How do we possess the woman of God's dreams for us? How do we get into a relationship with her in sanctification and in an honorable way? First of all, if you want to find the right person, you have to first be the right kind of a person.

That is easy to say, but much harder to do. You need to be the right person. You need to check yourself out and inspect your own life. You need to be open to what God wants to do in your life.

Many times we talk a good talk, but we have such a hard time ever looking in the mirror at ourselves. It is difficult. It is much easier to see what is wrong in other people and tell them how to correct it. But God wants you to be concerned about working on yourself.

If someone is called to preach, then the first thing they must do is prepare. You don't just go out and pastor a church. You are not ready. Likewise, the call to marry and to find the right person is a call to be the right person.

For those of you already married, the same thing is true. The biggest problem in marriages is really not the person you married—it is YOU! But you are busy deflecting what God is trying to do in your life by looking at your spouse and figuring out what is wrong with them. You are blinded to you own sin.

When a young man begins to think that the time is right and God wants him to get married, that is a call to be the right person. The call to marriage is the call to manage your own life.

In Genesis 2:18, God saw the need for Adam to have a helpmeet. So God got involved. He brought all the animals by but saw that there were none that were suitable. Then God put Adam to sleep, and when God woke him up, Adam had a bride.

Who saw the need? God did. From all indications in Genesis, Adam wasn't unhappy at all. He was quite happy in the garden and didn't have a problem. God saw that he needed more than an animal. He needed a wife.

Fathers, when your sons get to the place where they are marriageable, then you can approach him and let him know that it is time to start looking. You might have to wake him up if he is still asleep—and there is nothing wrong with that.

How can you tell if your son is ready to be married? Think, "Would I marry my daughter to a boy like my son?" That is how you can know if he is ready or not. If the answer is No, then you know there is more work he needs to do in his life.

I find it interesting that in Ruth's life, it was Naomi that saw the need for her to get married. This is an interesting principle. Her godly mother-in-law saw the need and suggested to Ruth that she needed to start thinking about getting married. Then she told her about Boaz and instructed her on how to go about presenting herself to him.

In Genesis 2:24 the Bible lays out this principle—a man is to leave his father and mother and cleave to his wife. The picture is this—the young man, until the moment that he goes to cleave to his wife, is with father and mother.

As that young man is getting older, he is getting more independent, but he should not cut off his ties with his parents until the day that he gets married. That gives him an accountability relationship.

Parents, you need to be involved with your kids at this stage in their life. You need to be there, teaching them how to evaluate their own life. They are often way too young and cannot see the areas of life that they need to make changes in. As parents, you can see those areas of weakness and help them to recognize them.

Character Qualities

One of the best ways to know when your young person is ready for marriage is to look at character qualities in your child's life.

I have developed a character quality worksheet to help you to be able to rate your young person in different areas. This character quality worksheet is available as a printable PFD at this link: *www. purposedcoachingblog.com/CharacterQualitiesCheckList.pdf.*

Have your son or daughter complete the worksheet and rate themselves in these areas. Then you as the parents should each fill out a worksheet evaluating your son or daughter. Then the three of you need to sit down and compare notes. That will give you a more accurate overall picture.

Young people, if you will do this with your parents, you will be able to recognize the areas that you are weak in and areas that you need to grow in. Parents, if your evaluation is very different from your young person's evaluation, then there is a perspective issue that needs to be addressed. They don't have a realistic view of themselves. Or you have not been honest in your evaluation of them.

After you have finished the worksheets and compared notes, then go back and pick the top 5 that are your strongest character qualities. Those are the character qualities that you want to build on in your life. Then pick out the 5 worst character qualities and those are the ones you need to work on and try to bring them up.

This can be a powerful tool for you and your parents to help you grow in the area of character, and to be able to assess if you are ready for marriage. Let me give you a word of warning. If you and your parents are not honest when you fill out the worksheet, it will not give you an accurate picture.

If you rate yourself too low, it will only discourage you. If you rate yourself too high, it will give you a wrong perspective of your character.

Parents, you need to be honest too. Don't stick your head in the sand and pretend that your son or daughter has no weaknesses. We all have weaknesses, and we all have strengths. Be sure to give an honest evaluation.

Consistent Growth

Second Corinthians 3:18 tells us where we are headed in all this. *"But we all with open face beholding as in a glass the glory of the Lord, are changed into the same image from glory to glory, even as by the Spirit of the Lord."*

You are raising a young man or young lady who is to be changed by the Spirit of the Lord. Therefore, you ought to be able to see some marked growth taking place over time. They should be able to see it in their own life as well.

There ought to be marked changes in them that can be seen. There should be an attitude adjustment, an over-all awareness, and a striving for excellence in their life.

The goal is not just to build character qualities, but to have a good over-all character of life. Young people, you need to be growing in your relationship with the Lord and in your relationship with your parents. Character is a consistent predictable choice in life that you can expect out of a person.

For instance, one of the character qualities listed one the sheet is alertness. If your child is alert, they are paying attention to what is going on. They are aware of what is taking place around them.

If have someone strong in the area of alertness, and you asked them to describe a situation, they will be able to give you the answer. Someone who is not alert is a person caught in unawareness, like a zombie. If you ask them to describe the same situation, they will have no idea what happened.

Marriage is going to amplify your strong character qualities, but it is going to take your weak character qualities and drag them down further. Young ladies, can you imagine marrying a guy that is unaware of what is going on around them? Marriage is going to make him even more unaware and cause problems in your marriage.

If that is going to bother you, you need to know that before you marry a guy like that. If that is going to bother you, young man, you better know that before you get married. You need to work on those weak areas.

That is why it becomes so very critical in the assessment stage for you to understand something about the family out of which the young lady or the young man is coming that you are about to marry. We will talk more about this when we get to the assessment stage. But how they interact as a family will have a major impact on how your future spouse is going to treat you.

You need to pay attention. Ladies, you need to notice how the young man's father treats his mother and how they get along. I am not saying that is exactly how your future husband will treat you, but he will definitely be influenced by the way his parents interact. And that is probably what you are going to face in the future. So you need to be well warned ahead of time.

Parents, you better check out that guy they are going to marry and make sure that he knows how to interact and make wise decisions. If he is proud and cocky and runs off and does his own thing, you better yank your daughter out of that relationship in a hurry. He is going to be big trouble down the road.

As you identify the weaknesses in your son or daughter and then start working on those areas, you should be able to see some marked improvement and see them moving in a good direction. This will help you to be able to assess whether or not they are ready for marriage, or whether there are more areas they need to work on.

Parents, it is also your job to teach your son or your daughter how to assess themselves, using the character qualities sheet. This is also a great time and place to start evaluating the character of others. However, I am not suggesting that you go through the church and pick out different young people and evaluate them to see if they would make a good husband or a good wife.

You need to stay away from evaluating church people. Let me tell you why. If you start doing that, you will turn your young person into a critical person. They will go around judging everyone and speaking against those they don't like. That is not Christian and it is not right.

There have been a lot of young ladies that turned their noses up at some guy, and the parents agreed with her evaluation. Then later she turns around and marries the guy. Boys have a way of changing and growing up and maturing. The girl that thought he was just a complete idiot one day wakes up and recognizes that he has changed a lot.

But I do suggest that you do this kind of evaluation from a distance—maybe the kids in the neighborhood or relatives or friends that you know from other places and their kids. You are not going to delve into every detail, but by doing an evaluation of character, you will help your young person learn to start sorting out character qualities in other people's lives. It will help them to learn why that makes them a good candidate for marriage or a bad candidate for marriage.

You can begin pointing out good character qualities in young people in the church, and even old people in the church. Pick out some older people that are married and evaluate them. Help your young person to see why they are doing so well together as a husband and a wife. Point out good character qualities.

Let me give you one example of how this can be done. A young man got interested in a young lady that was in another church and another state. The son was marriageable age and ready to married, and was looking for the right young lady. So he and his father decided to go visit the church where the young lady was a member.

They never told the young lady or her parents or anyone else in the church that they were coming, or what their purpose in being there was. They stayed at the church for a week, offering their services to help with different projects around the church. They attended every service and every activity at the church, interacting and intermingling with people in the church. They were especially watching the young lady and her parents.

At the end of the week, they packed their bags and they left. They had determined that the young lady was of sterling character, but they also knew that there was more to evaluate than just character.

Just because a person has good character does not mean that they are a good match for your son or your daughter. Character is probably the most important piece of all, but it is not the only thing that needs to be evaluated.

After being at the church all week, they determined that the young lady was not a good match for the young man, so they left quietly, and the young lady never knew. She didn't have to get her hopes up or get her heart broken.

All of your evaluating cannot be done that way, but a major piece of it can. There can be some very fine young people with good character, but they just are not a good match for your son or daughter. That kind of evaluating can be done somewhat from a distance.

Considerations

Young people, if you are in this alert stage, there are four different things you need to consider.

First, *get into an accountability relationship with your parents and start working on your own character.* Find the areas that are weak and work on building up those areas.

Second, *start learning how to evaluate and look at character qualities in other people, and how to pick out the good ones.* As you are learning how to pick out the best character qualities, you are learning how to discern whether this person would be a good candidate for marriage.

Third, *pray.* Isn't that a novel idea! I am of the opinion that God has one lady for one man. God knows exactly who you are to marry. Out of the all the women in the world, I believe that God chose my wife for me. He didn't do it because I was smart enough to figure it out. He did it in spite of my dumbness.

Let me just tell you. If you can be as dumb as I was and wind up with the right wife, surely if you would start praying and asking God, He could give you the right wife.

You might not know where you are going to find her—but you only need one. There are several billion people on the earth. If I was going to go looking for the right one, I wouldn't know where to start—but God knows.

And God knows how to bring her across your path, and bring her attention to you. God knows how to make those connections to happen. Pray and seek God's face—He can do it.

Fourth, *trust God*. Ultimately, this is all about God at work in your life and directing your path. If you marry the wrong girl or the wrong guy, it is going to have forever impact on your life.

Marriage is the second most important decision that you will ever make, behind the issue of salvation. Therefore, it is the first and most important decision humanly speaking that you will ever make in this life. Who will you marry? So in this area, waiting on God is really a wise choice.

Chapter Four
Step Three—The Approach

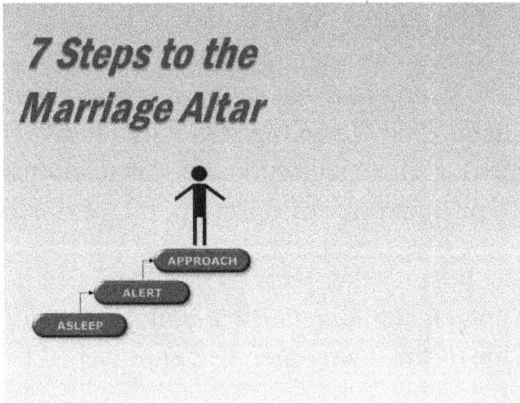

Once a young man has come to the place where he believes he is ready for marriage, and his parents think he is ready, he begins to look for the right young lady. Soon God focuses his attention on a certain young lady, so he begins to pray about whether she is the right one. He asks his parents to pray with him about this certain young lady also.

After some time of seeking God's will, the parents and the young man believe that this certain girl is the right one. How does he then approach the parents of the young lady? That is what this third step is about—how the young man approaches the parents of the young lady.

The young man is the initiator

Let me mention a couple of things here. First of all, it is the young man that is the initiator in this process. It is not the young lady that goes looking for a young man. The young lady is to also be praying about the young man that God has for her to marry, but she needs to be waiting for God to bring that young man into her life.

The son becomes the one who makes the approach for the young lady. Proverbs 18:22 reminds us of this principle. *"Whoso findeth a wife findeth a good thing, and obtaineth favour of the LORD."* Notice it says *he* that finds a wife, not *she* that finds a husband.

The very job and responsibility of finding a wife and taking a wife is upon the shoulders of the young man, not the young lady. That does not mean that the young lady has nothing to do with any of this, but it does mean that it is on the young man's shoulders. Therefore he is the one that needs to take the initiative in this relationship. He needs to be willing to pay the price of rejection, if that should happen.

I was talking with a preacher recently who said that he had a young lady from his church attending a Bible college that does not believe in betrothal. One of the young men had approached her and wanted to date her.

She told him she was sorry that she did not date, but he needed to call her father and talk with him. The young man said, "It is not worth that much trouble."

The pastor wisely told her, "He just told you what he thinks of you—that you are not worth that much trouble." Young ladies, if the young man will not deal with your parents, then he is not worth your time at all. In fact, I think it would be appropriate to kick him in the shins as you walk away.

Parents Need to be Involved

Second, I want to point out that the young man needs to seek the will of God through God-ordained authority. I have seen a young man before that decided what girl he wanted, without seeking his parent's counsel.

But when he went to talk to the parents of the young lady, they said no. The young man got angry and upset, thinking he had found the will of God.

That young man needs to realize that God works through God-ordained authority. If you don't work through your parents, you will cause heartbreak and problems.

God has put authorities in our lives for a reason. There are some issues that come up in this area, but over-all if you have Christian parents you ought to be working with them and submitting to their authority in your life.

The approach can be done in a number of ways. It could be the parents that go talk to the parents. It could be the young man that goes and talks with the father. It could be the young man that goes and talks to both the father and the mother of the young lady.

It could be that the parents and the young man go and talk to the parents of the young lady. It could be that the young man and his father go talk to the father.

So you see there could be a variety of approaches that are made, and none of them are necessarily wrong. But the approach is always first to the parents, and they have the responsibility of making some assessment.

Obviously because the son first of all is under the authority of his parents, the approach needs to be made with his parent's permission. The parents need to believe that the son is ready for marriage and has the right character.

Then the young man, recognizing the young lady is under authority as well, should never approach the young lady, but rather her parents. Talking to the young lady first only sets her up to have a broken heart. The young man approaches the father of the young lady, because she is under his authority.

Young lady, what do you do if a young man approaches you and lets you know he is interested in you? You should tell him to go speak to your father.

Personally, I would never consider such a young man for my daughter. If he does not have the courage to approach me and ask for permission first, he is not worthy of my daughter.

Examples in the Word of God

The Bible contains very few examples of how this approach is done. Again, let me say to you that we are not talking about rules, but rather how to make sure whatever we do is under the umbrella of these principles. Let's looks at some of the ways that the approach was made in the Bible.

Isaac

In Genesis chapter twenty-four, Isaac wanted a bride, so his father decided to send Eliezer his trusted servant back to the home country to find a bride. He sent him with strict instructions of what she was to be like and where to find her.

When Eliezer found Rebekah, he first approached her parents. When they agreed to the marriage, then Rebekah was given the right of refusal and she chose to accept the proposal. So Eliezer took her back to Isaac and she became his wife.

So we see that certain situations may require some unusual ways of operating. I am not suggesting that to be the best, but sometimes in certain situation we have to make some adjustments. That is what happened with Isaac.

Jacob

In Genesis chapter twenty-nine we find the story of Jacob who was heading back to his mother's family to find a wife. His parents had given him some guidelines to follow, but his parents were not there with him. He ended up paying a price in order to marry Rachel, when he had to serve for 14 years.

Of course, we know that he worked for 7 years and then got Leah instead of Rachel. So he served 7 more years for his beloved Rachel. Now I don't recommend two wives.

Just because they did it in Bible days does not mean it is necessarily OK. In the New Testament the Bible says that God winked at some things that were done. It doesn't mean it was OK—it is just what happened.

Put yourself in Leah's shoes. Your father has substituted you without telling the groom. He finds out who you are on his wedding night, and the very next morning he goes to your father and complain, "That's not the one I wanted to marry. How long do I have to serve you to get the one that I want?"

Then you are married to him for 7 more years while he has a heart that is pining for the next wife to come. Imagine being thrown into a family mess like that. Jacob got into a big mess, partly because his parents were not involved. If they had been there, they might have been able to warn him.

Ruth

Then we have the story of Ruth who was given instruction by her mother-in-law on how to present herself to Boaz. Those 3 events are the sum total in the Old Testament of people who were getting married and how those approaches were made. In all 3, there are unusual events and circumstances.

There are going to be times when a young man and a young lady get married, and they don't keep all the principles. In fact, just about everybody that gets to the marriage altar has violated those principles to some degree or another.

But that doesn't mean we throw the principles out and forget them. We should do what we can to guard the principles. We do not want to violate the principles of the Word of God in getting to the marriage altar. If we violate God's principles, we will end up sowing seeds of destruction in our own marriage.

Daughters are given in marriage

My daughter is under my authority until she gets married. According to the Word of God, the young lady is given in marriage. In our marriage ceremony, this is demonstrated by the words, "Who gives this woman in marriage?" And the father replies, "Her mother and I do."

So as a father, it is my responsibility to deliver my daughter to that marriage altar and to give her away. And I need to be sure that when I do that, I have cared for her as she ought to be cared for, until that day arrives. She is my responsibility.

Does that mean that a daughter could never move out of the house? No, but even if she does, she is still under her dad's authority. As she gets older, she may gather a little more independence but she still needs to be responsive to her parents. She is still under their authority until the marriage takes place.

The young man however, has the responsibility of being the initiator in this approach. He is being raised to take on independence and to be the head of his own home someday. He ought to be willing to take the risk of asking for the girl's hand in marriage.

Young men, let me warn you that there are going to be times when you are going to ask for the girl's hands, and the parents are going to say no. How should you respond? You need to take it like a man. Don't go around pouting and being upset.

You might not understand why they turned you down. But that's OK—you don't need to know. It may have absolutely nothing to do with whether they like you or not. It has to do with whether or not they believe you are God's choice for their daughter. And that is their responsibility to make that choice.

Parents, I recommend that you never tell your daughter about the young man's request if you turn him down. She does not need to know unless he is a suitable candidate. If he is a young man that she sees from time to time, she will feel very awkward anytime she is around him after that. If she doesn't know about it, it will not make her feel awkward.

Daughters are given in marriage. The father then is responsible for that girl's purity. That is why he should be approached. The approach is to the parents of the girl—not to the girl directly. The risk that takes place is all on the shoulders of the young man.

Praying for God's Will

As the young man makes the approach to the parents of the young lady, he needs to be praying. Pray that God will work out all the details. Pray that if she is the right one, her parents will be in agreement. Pray that her heart would be open to the will of God for her life. The parents of the young man also need to be praying for God's will in the matter.

How do the parents of the young lady know that this young man is the right one for their daughter? They too need to pray about whether or not this is God's will. They need wisdom to know whether or not to speak to their daughter about this young man that has approached them.

Parents, let me just say that if the young man that doesn't have high character, you would not even want to present him to your daughter. If he is a guy that is constantly having wrecks and breaking the law speeding, are you going to put your daughter in that kind of a situation? That is not what I want for my daughter.

What if he is a young man that hops around from job to job and can't keep a job, or gets fired from jobs all the time? Nope, that is not the kind of young man that I am interested in for my daughter. I will be looking for some kind of financial security in the young man that wants to marry my daughter.

What if he is a young man that isn't faithful in the house of God or doesn't serve the Lord? Sorry, but that is an important consideration for me. I would not even consider such a young man for my daughter.

So you see, there are just some real common things that you can look at and eliminate some guys very quickly. You don't even have to pray about it. They are not even quality enough that I would begin to consider them for my young lady.

Young man, your character is being watched. Right now, you don't care what people think—you just want to have a good time. But one day, you may wish that somebody thought well of you. Due to your foolishness in the past, you lost your opportunity. Pay attention to your walk with God. There is a payoff later on.

Young ladies, the same goes the other way around for you. If you go out and mess around and throw your life away, you will regret it later. You will wonder why the parents of some young man don't think that you are the right young lady for him. The way you respond and behave is important.

Church members, let me encourage you to be praying for the young ladies and young men in your church. As they are going about the whole process of asking God for His will and for the right person to marry, you and I as God's people ought to make it our responsibility to be praying seriously and earnestly for them. Pray that they would know God's will and find just the person God wants them to marry.

Conclusion

I love watching a marriage where God has put it all together. As two people begin to mesh and mold together with each other, and begin to raise their kids and live for Christ, it is a beautiful thing. As far as I am concerned, they are just amazing specimens of what God can do in young people's lives that are yielded to him.

Sadly, we have all seen tragic examples of what happens when you do things your way. My goal is to never have another one of those.

I know I am not going to be able to get it done totally, because I am not the only one voting! But that is my goal.

So let's pray for our young people—for God to bring the right young man and the right young lady together. Out of all the people on planet earth, God knows that they belong to each other. Together they can build a family that will serve and honor Jesus Christ.

It is the young man that is the initiator in this process. It is not the young lady that goes looking for a young man.

The young lady is to also be praying about the young man that God has for her to marry, but she needs to be waiting for God to bring that young man into her life.

Chapter Five
Step Four—Assessment

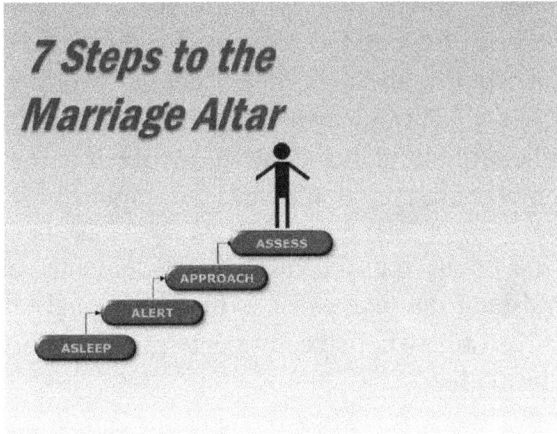

7 Steps to the Marriage Altar

We come now to the next step which is the assessment. During the assessment step, the character of the young man or the young lady is evaluated. Is this person the right one to marry my son or daughter?

The assessment step can be done before the approach or after the approach, whichever one is best in the situation. If a full assessment can be made before the approach, then that is how it should be done.

If however, it is two people that don't each other well and the parents don't know each other, then there needs to be an assessment period after the approach. The parents of the young lady will need to make an assessment of the character of the young man to determine if he is a good match for their daughter.

If the young man and his parents have determined that a certain young lady is the right one for him, then the young man makes the approach. He goes to ask the parents of the young lady if he can marry their daughter.

Now the father and mother of the young lady begin to consider the young man. They make an assessment of him. The parents check out the young man's character and decide whether or not the young man is the one for their daughter.

There are many questions that go through the mind of a father at this time. "What if I check the guy out, decide he is OK, and he is not OK? What do I do then? What if I get the wrong guy in there? What if I send the right guy away?" Because of that, there are a lot of parents who will sit back and not be involved in the life of their young person because they don't want the responsibility.

Obviously, the young man has already made some assessment as he has been asking the question, "Is this young lady the right one for me?" He has done what he can to determine the character of the young lady from afar.

Young men, if you can make a thorough assessment without even approaching the parents of the young lady, it is best. Then if you decide that the young lady is not the girl for you, there are no hurt feelings in the matter.

But if such an assessment cannot be made, then it has to be made after the approach. Or if you have assessed all you can from afar, there comes a point that you have to say, "I know the young lady well enough up to a point, but I don't know enough to know if she is the right one." That usually happens because of distance.

Now it becomes the job of the parents of the young lady to make an assessment of the young man. Parents, this assessment is done before you ever go to your daughter and tell her of the young man's interest in her. You first clear the young man's character.

Parents have veto power at this point if they realize that the young man does not have the right kind of character or if they realize that his personality would not mesh well with their daughter. Fathers, don't say, "Let me talk to my daughter and if she likes you, we will talk about it." No, you check out the young man first before you approach your daughter.

You may have to ask the young man to come to where you are for a while so you can get to know him better. If he is not willing to spend time with you answering your questions, and showing you his character, then he is not worthy of your daughter. It is that simple.

Parents have a responsibility to assess his character as best they can. But they are not the final say on whether the young man is the right one. The young lady has the final say in that matter.

Parents aren't the final judge. They are just meant to be a guard in the situation to keep the young lady's heart from being hurt and to keep this situation from going to a place of danger in case this young man is not the right one.

So the assessment is on both sides. The young lady has every right to say no, even if her parents approve of his character and are OK with him. She needs to assess the young man and determine whether or not she thinks he is the right kind of a young man for her to marry.

Begins with Character

Assessment begins with character. We talked about that a little bit in the last chapter with the perceived character qualities worksheet. My recommendation would be that you go through these character qualities, assessing your own strengths and weaknesses. The worksheet is available in printable PDF format at this link: ***http://www.purposedcoachingblog.com/CharacterQualitiesCheckList.pdf.***

Young men, after you and your parents have assessed your character in these areas and you are ready for marriage, one of the ways that you can begin to assess character in the young lady you are interested in is to determine how you would rate her character in those forty-nine areas.

The areas that are poor go in one pile, the areas that are good in another pile, and the ones that you are unsure of in the middle. If there are more than 10 areas that you are unsure of, then you don't know her well enough to say, "This is the young lady for me to marry."

In most marriages that take place, young people have never even thought about the character qualities in the person they are marrying. They don't even stop to consider it until well after the marriage has taken place.

Then the problems begin to happen, and you say, "Oh no, what have I done to myself?" I highly recommend this assessment. It will help you as you begin to take a look at your own character and then the character of the young lady.

The young lady and her parents also need to sit down and do an assessment on the young man. Do we know this young man well enough to say that he is the right one for our daughter? Can we look at these character qualities and see them in operation in his life.

Don't settle on character qualities that you assume are present. Make sure that you are dealing with character qualities that you can show are present. There is a big difference. Just because a young man goes to church and is active and even serves in the church, does not necessarily mean that his character is godly in every area.

Don't assume anything. I recommend that as you look at the character qualities, you go through the different areas and ask yourself, "How do I see alertness being show in this person's life? What story could I tell about this person's life that shows this character quality being exhibited?"

If you will go through each area and ask yourself that question, you will have a good idea if you really know the person well enough to make a wise decision. Don't just assume you know the young man well. You need to ask questions.

Proverbs 31:10-31 tell us that a virtuous woman is hard to find. Where does God put the emphasis in what you ought to be looking for when you are looking for a young lady? In that passage, God lists her virtues, or her character. Does she have character?

What do most guys look for? They go for looks—is she good looking and flashy? Does she faun over me? Does she flirt with me? Young men, you need to beware. Many girls have good looks, but they have a great lack of Godly character.

The Bible tells us that the virtuous woman is hard to find. Her character is described in Proverbs 31 and in other places throughout the Word of God. God also says that her price is far above rubies. She is worth more than all the money that you could ever amass. You will never be able to pay for her.

The Bible also talks about the character qualities that a young man ought to possess if he is to marry. Ladies, when you are assessing the young man, don't look for lots of muscles and good looks—look for character.

When you let emotions and feelings get in the middle of your assessment, everything else goes out the window. You can't do a proper character assessment, because your feelings become the most important part of your judgment. That will destroy you when it comes to determining character.

God says in Proverbs 28:26, *"He that trusteth in his own heart is a fool: but whoso walketh wisely, he shall be delivered."* That verse is very applicable to the way many in our society go about finding a wife. We should be trying in every way possible to keep emotions out of the picture.

We mentioned the principle earlier that romance belongs in a committed relationship. You need to guard yourself so you don't let your emotions get involved in the process of assessment. You are to be judging character. If you let emotions get involved, it will destroy your ability to make a wise decision.

Sometimes people are concerned that they will decide to marry each other, but then they can't love each other. Well, let me just tell you, there has never yet been two godly people locked in a commitment to each other who have not been able to fall in love.

Love is more about choice and about commitment than it is about some kind of a feeling or an emotion. The emotion will always follow. That won't be a problem.

When people begin to feel all excited and all woozy about another person, the ability to assess character is gone. Their clear thinking runs out the window. You may very well regret the decision that you made when the fire goes out after the marriage.

Areas to Consider

After you have looked at the person's character, here are some other areas to consider in your assessment. The biggest concern as you are making these assessments needs to be a matter of the heart (First Peter 3:4). Where is the heart of the individual? That is what you are really assessing.

Profession

It is important that both the young man and the young lady know Christ as their Lord and Savior. Does she have a profession? What about his profession? Do they both know Christ?

Second Corinthians 6:14 says that there should not be an unequal yoke. Many a young lady has gone out, done her fishing looking for a young man, and found a guy that is not saved. She thinks that he wants her so bad that he will become a Christian.

She gets him maybe to even pray a prayer and come to church some. But as soon as the knot is tied, they wind up in trouble in their marriage. Eventually they wind up in divorce court. Don't think that you can go against the Word of God and everything will work out OK.

As Christians, we are to marry in the Lord (First Corinthians 7:39). We should never use the bait of, "I would marry you if you were a Christian," to get someone to become a professing Christian. Their profession will not be genuine.

But more importantly, we want to know what their doctrine is. They don't need to be a theologian, but they should living out what they say they believe. If they are not living for Christ, you need to pass them over.

Many young men have made a profession of salvation to please a young lady. They may even get baptized and start going to church. Let me tell you, any young man can do that for a few years, and act like they are a Christian. Then as soon as they get the knot tied and they are off on their own, they take their sweetheart and head another direction.

That young lady is left in a miserable marriage, raising children that have a divided home. It ought not to happen, but it can happen, and it does happen. Young ladies allow their emotions to get ahead of character assessment and they wind up in trouble.

Pursuit

We are looking here for a young man and a young lady that shows direction in their life. It is vital for the girl to know about the young man and to know which way he will lead the family. Is he being led, or is he doing the leading?

If the young lady has to grab him by the nose and pull him along, there will come a day when he gets tired of being pulled by the nose. He will have enough and be fed up, and he will finally draw the line. You will have marriage trouble. I don't recommend going into a marriage that way.

Are they pursuing the things of the Lord? Do they have the mind of Christ and are they concerned about the things of God? How does he/she use the Bible to make their decisions?

Here is a good question to ask: What was the last major decision that you made? How did the Bible play into that decision? Give me some examples of how you made a decision biblically. If they have to sit there and scramble for an answer, you know that the Bible didn't have a part in their decision.

I recommend that when you are asking these kinds of questions, be careful how you word them. Don't just ask, "Do you use the Bible to make your decisions?" He can easily answer yes to that kind of a question.

Instead ask, "How do you use the Bible to make your decisions? Give me an example of using the Bible to make a decision. When was the last time and how did it play out?" Those kinds of questions will help you find out the real truth.

Partnership

Do his/her actions match their words? Do they do what they say? What do they think in the areas of education, work, family, recreation, politics, friends, and finances? These are all areas that are very vital and important in life, and they should not be left to chance. You need to know these things before you move into a relationship.

In Amos 3:3, God asks the question, ***"Can two walk except they be agreed?"*** How do you get to know whether or not you agree? The best way to find out is to ask some good questions.

I have put together a booklet entitled, ***Questions to ask in Preparation for Betrothal***. These can be used by both the young man and the young lady during this assessment process. You can download a printable PDF of that booklet at this link: ***http://www. purposedcoachingblog.com/QuestionsforBetrothal.pdf.***

Let me make something clear. I do not recommend that you use ALL the questions. There are too many. You could be busy for the next year asking these questions. If you are a father, and you want to keep the guy from marrying your daughter, that would be a good way to do it. You can probably make it so uncomfortable for him that he will go the other way eventually.

But I don't recommend doing it that way. If you are going to let him down, be honest and clear with him and let him know it probably isn't going to work. That is much better than letting it drag on and on and then letting him down.

There are certain questions in the list that the father of a young lady should be asking of the young man. Go through and mark twenty to thirty of the most important questions that you want to ask him.

For example, here is one of the questions. Would you raise your children the way you were raised? You can elaborate on that by then asking: if no, what was wrong with the way you were raised and what would you change? If yes, tell me what was good about the way you were raised?

The way he answers those questions will tell you a lot about the young man. Many marriages have difficulties because the wife thinks the kids should be raised one way, and the husband thinks they should be raised another way. It will cause a big clash and a major battle, and may even lead to divorce.

Here is another question: would you rather be at home or hang out with your friends? Tell me about how that is going to play out in the marriage. Tell me about why you want to hang out with your friends all the time instead of spending time with your parents.

If you are looking at a young man that always wants to hang out with his friends and he doesn't want to be with his family, it is probably a good indicator that he is not going to want to be home with his wife and kids. I would want to know that up front before my daughter winds up with some guy that won't be around, and expects her to take care of everything while he goes and enjoys himself.

There are a number of powerful and insightful questions in the booklet that ought to be asked. There are questions that deal with physical issues, questions that deal with emotional issues, and questions that deal with spiritual issues. Each of those areas is an important area to explore.

Some people don't think that the physical issue needs to be discussed, but it is important as well. I had a father awhile back who called me from another state. He had a daughter who had some pretty serious physical problems, which will mean some very expensive surgery and medical care going forward. It could even mean an early death for his daughter.

He wanted the name of a young man. Before I gave him any names, I asked him, "Are you going to let the young man know about your daughter's physical issues?" He got very upset that I would ask such a question, and let me know that it was not anyone else's business.

I couldn't believe that he would hide something like that from a young man. Obviously, I didn't pass the name on. If my daughter were like that, I would want the young man to know ahead of time what to expect and what he is going to face in the future. It is going to be a big expense and he needs to be prepared for that.

He also needs to know about the possibility of an early death. If the young man loves the young lady and is willing to make that kind of a sacrifice, that is wonderful. But he needs to know about it up front—not find it out after the fact. He needs to know these things before he makes his decision to marry the young lady.

These are some very powerful questions that can be a great help to you if you will use them right. As a father of a young lady, those questions should be asked of the young man. Then the young lady also needs to ask those questions of the young man.

I know of a young lady who used many of these questions in this booklet. She asked the young man that was interested in her these questions. She put him through the third degree.

When it was all over with, she had found that he was headed in the right direction. Both she and her parents agreed that he was the right one. They went in with their eyes wide open. What she actually said to her future husband was, "You thought my dad's questions were tough. I have to warn you—my questions are a lot harder."

When it was all over, he said, "You were right. Your questions were a lot harder than your dad's questions." Young ladies, I would recommend that it be that way—you are going to have to be stuck with the turkey the rest of your life! You need to know what you are getting into.

Why would I call a young man a turkey? Well, I know a lot of young men, and I think turkey pretty well describes them. The other word that I use sometimes to describe them is gorilla. You can choose whatever word you like.

If the young man and a young lady live far apart in different places, and they don't know each other very well, they could use these questions to get to know each other better. They need to be sure that they keep romance and emotions out of it.

Remember, you are looking at character. She needs to know his character and he needs to know her character. You can use these questions to be able to do that.

Financial stability

This is an important issue to discuss. There are financial questions in the booklet, and I strongly recommend that you ask those. The young man ought to be willing to lay out examples of how he handles his finances.

If a young man will not handle his finances right, he has no business marrying your daughter. If he is not faithful in the little things, then he will not be counted worthy of the larger things in life, as far as God is concerned (Luke 16:10-11).

If a guy can't control his spending or he doesn't pay his bills on time, if he doesn't know how to tithe and he won't give to God—and he isn't doing all that before he goes to talk to the young lady, the young lady ought to tell him good-bye. You are out of here. I am done with you.

If he isn't faithful in the little things, I can only tell you it is going to be a horrible life for that young lady. She is worth a whole lot more than rubies and much more than money in the bank. If he can't handle the money in the bank, he isn't going to handle the young lady well and treat her with respect either.

Pleasantness

Physical

I am often asked the question, "Do I have to marry someone who is ugly? Do I have to marry this guy who is homely?" No, you do not. In fact, I recommend that you marry someone that you find attractive.

And let me just say that attractive is in the mind of the beholder. I mean, just look around. You don't have to look very far. Some of you guys—your wife married you and she has done you a great favor. But thankfully somehow God has put blinders on her and she thinks you are good looking, and you are happy to have her fooled.

In First Corinthians 7:3 the Bible is very clear that marriage is a physical relationship. This business of prudishness and pretending that marriage is not sexual is not Biblical. There is a joyful sexual tension to a marriage.

The bride is to adorn herself to make herself look beautiful. Ladies, there is nothing wrong with looking pretty for your husband. (Isaiah 61:10, 62:5). Abraham married a beautiful woman, and even the Egyptians shared that opinion about Sarah. Isaac married a beautiful woman. Jacob married a beautiful woman.

Christian modesty does not require that a woman look homely. I would park there for a while, but I think I am going to save it for a marriage message later. But ladies, let me tell you, you don't have to look homely just to be called Christian.

Mental and Intellectual

There is not only physical attraction to consider, but also mental and intellectual attraction. Are they going to get along? I don't recommend that a young man marry a young lady who is mentally way under him, nor do I recommend that a young man marry a young lady that is mentally way above him.

You need to be somewhat on par mentally and intellectually. Now, there will be areas where you are going to know a whole lot more than she does. There are also going to be areas where she knows a lot more than you do. The two of you can complement each other.

But you need to be able to be somewhat on the same intelligence level and able to engage each other in conversation. If that can't happen, you are going to find that you will soon run out of reason to enjoy the company of one another.

Emotional

I think you should seek a woman who agrees with you. Marriage is not to be run by emotion, but emotion should be a part of marriage. It won't always be, because emotions come and go, but you should be seeking a woman who agrees with you.

Don't marry someone that grates on you all the time. She will be fine for someone else, but she shouldn't have to be saddled with you. You will not love her like you should.

Ladies, there are 3 kinds of men and you need to assess this as you are looking at emotional attraction. The first kind of a man is an insecure man. He constantly has to propped up and reassured and patted on the back and told he is loved. Otherwise he goes away pouting. Stay away—you don't want a guy like that. He needs to grow up.

The second kind of a man is one that is confident in a fleshly way. He thinks he can just handle anything. Look out—he is headed for some major train wrecks in his life, and you are going to be part of the train wreck. If you really want to marry him, back off and wait until the train wrecks are over and see what he turns out like. Don't be along for the ride.

The third kind of a man is the kind you really want—a confident man who is confident in a godly way. He has found that he can walk with God and trust God.

Conclusion

The assessment step is a very important step. Remember you are looking at the character of the other person, to determine if they are the right one for you to marry. The assessment is always done with parental involvement to keep it from getting out of hand.

You don't want the emotions to start to play into the matter, because that can cause great damage if there is not going to be a marriage. The assessment is for the purpose of answering the question: do we want to go forward to marriage or not? Is this the young man/young lady that God would have for me to marry?

After you determine that you are right for each other and you have come to the point of agreement, then you can turn around and take the questions left over and deepen your relationship. It will help you to get to know each other far better.

Chapter Six
Step Five—Agreement

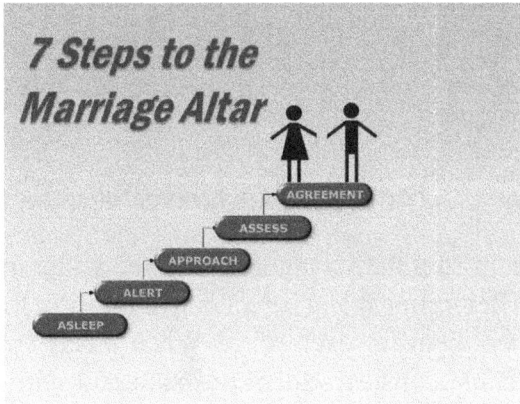

The fifth step is the Step of Agreement. In this step, an agreement is made between the young man, the young lady, and both sets of parents. This is where the betrothal takes place—the commitment is made to go to the marriage altar.

Betrothal is a subject that is not often preached on in many churches. In fact, it is often dismissed as not being for our day and age. It is rather humorous—if it were not so sad—that there are books written about Bible principles of dating, when dating never happened in the Bible. There are books about Bible principles of courtship, when courtship never happened in the Bible. Only betrothal ever did.

Now I am not going to argue for the name necessarily, because that is not the most important thing to consider when getting to the marriage altar. But there are 3 Bible principles—not rules but principles—that need to be woven into any part of our practice. If we are to get to the marriage altar in a right way, these principles will be found in whatever our practice may be.

I am not going to suggest to you that the seven steps that I am giving you are the only way to do things. I am just trying to give you some practical thoughts and some practical wisdom on how to do things in a way that will guard the three principles. What I am giving you are not rules, but practical wise advice.

When we come to scripture we find that betrothal is often spoken of and seen over and over again. For example, we see Isaac and Rebekah, Jacob and Rachel, and Jesus and His church. Betrothal was the way of getting to the marriage altar in Bible days, in both the Old and New Testament.

The Four-Way Agreement

In the agreement step the young lady and the young man and both sets of parents determine that it is God's will for them to marry—that God has chosen them for each other. When a betrothal agreement is made, the Bible considers them husband and wife at this point without any physical involvement with each other.

Let me show you why I say that the agreement process is a four-way process. In Genesis 2:24, the Bible says, *"Therefore shall a man leave his father and his mother, and shall cleave unto his wife: and they shall be one flesh."*

The young man is leaving his father and his mother, so obviously his father and mother are involved. Until he comes to cleave to his wife, her place is to be under the protection of her parents, especially her father, and her purity is to be guarded by him. Therefore, it is only reasonable to realize that this is a 4-way agreement, not a 2-way agreement.

It is not the parents of the girl and the parents of the boy deciding that the two young people are going to marry. That is an arranged marriage, and it is not Biblical. Both the young man and the young lady have veto power in this issue.

Neither is it the young man and young lady deciding they will get married, and then they go tell their parents. The Bible is very clear that the parents need to be involved in the whole issue as well—which means all 4 parties much agree before the marriage can go forward.

The honoring of parents comes into play here also (Exodus 20:12, Ephesians 6:2). Young people, you need to honor your parents in this situation. This is the second most important decision made in your life, therefore you certainly ought to be careful not to skirt around parental involvement. The father is to protect the daughter from rash and unwise vows (Numbers chapter 30) and to protect his daughter's purity (Deuteronomy chapter 22).

I want to say this clearly because some people think that betrothal is an arranged marriage. Betrothal is NOT an arranged marriage. The young lady has a right of choice in this matter and the right of refusal (Genesis 24:58).

Parents need to be very careful that in presenting a young man to a young lady that they do not overly exert pressure on her to force her into a place of marrying someone that she does not desire to marry. That is even a greater danger for a young lady than it is for a young man. Young men should at this point in time have enough ability to take responsibility on their shoulders, walk their own path, take their own stand, do what is right and express their own desires.

But a young lady will often be careful and concerned about saying no to parents, and if she is not careful she will go too far into the realm of pleasing them. By doing that, she will just go along with what her parents say, and wind up in an unhappy marriage. I do not recommend that at all.

The Bride Price

Along with agreement, one of the wise things to be able to do is the Bible practice of a Bride price (Genesis 24:53). I am not going to spend a lot of time on this. Neither am I going to say that you have to necessarily practice this.

But in the Bible a bride price was a gift given by the young man to the parents of the young lady. It was given for the purpose of being a pledge to the young lady. The bride price showed the young lady's parents that he recognized that it was a committed relationship.

He gave the gift to the father, and if something happened through the betrothal period that the marriage did not take place, when the young lady came back home she got that bride price to keep for herself. In other words, there was something of great value that he was going to forfeit if he broke the relationship.

Also, by giving that bride price, he is saying that he valued the young lady greatly. She was worth something great to him. If her price is far above rubies, like God says, you could never pay enough for her. It cost him something to give the bride price, but he was willing to sacrifice of himself for the young lady.

But think about that young lady. She has spent all her life growing up in her parent's home. Her father has protected her, cared for her, loved her, kept her secure, and now she is ready to step out into life in one of the most difficult arenas that there is.

I tell you, when I think about this, it is tough. The young lady is going to go marry the guy, and he says, "This is what we are going to do," and if she is going to follow the Bible, she will submit to him. What if he makes bad decisions? Let me remove the ifs, because he will make bad decisions. When he does, what is she to do?

Any man that is honest will admit that he has made bad decisions in his life. The woman he is married to has to live with that. As a guy, I make bad decisions and I have to live with them too, but I have no one to blame but myself. My wife has me to blame.

Young man, by giving a bride price, you are saying to the father of this young lady, "I am asking you to entrust your daughter to me as a wife. I want you to know that I value her highly."

The young man I am going to give my daughter to will be a young man that values my daughter highly. If he doesn't value her, he is not going to get near her. That is just the way it is, because I care about my daughter. Any father who has any concern for his daughter wants to know that the man who is going to marry her is going to care for her as well or better than he has.

Let me just tell you, young men, the mindset of a father. One day you will understand. There is no young man that will take care of my daughter like I think is good enough. I am coming to that conclusion more and more.

To the young lady, the bride price says, "He values me highly." It begins a relationship of security, a sense that she is loved and cared for. She knows she is honored and she is going to be cherished. What young lady would not want that in a relationship?

Do you want some guy that is going to take you, use you, abuse you, and kick you to the curb? And you go through that 5, 10, or 20 times before you find the right one? Is that where you want to live, ladies? I don't think so.

I think a young lady who does not pay attention to this process and the Biblical teaching of the right way to get to the marriage altar is putting herself in a place of serious danger, and of great insecurity for the rest of her life. It may turn out OK, but it very well may not.

Who else paid the bride price in the Bible? How about Adam? He paid with one of his ribs. I don't think Adam was sorry about it at all. Did you hear what Adam said when Eve slipped up next to him, rubbing her hand over his ribs and feeling each rib? He looked over at her and said, "Honey, really, there is nobody else."

So the young man is paying a price to say to the young lady, "I want you to know I value you. I am putting my treasure where my heart is. And my heart is going where my treasure is. I am paying for you because I value you that much."

*From the point of agreement on is
where the romance comes into play.*

*Now the young man begins to woo and
to romance his young lady,
writing love notes, sending roses,
buying her special gifts.*

Chapter Seven
Step Six--Attraction

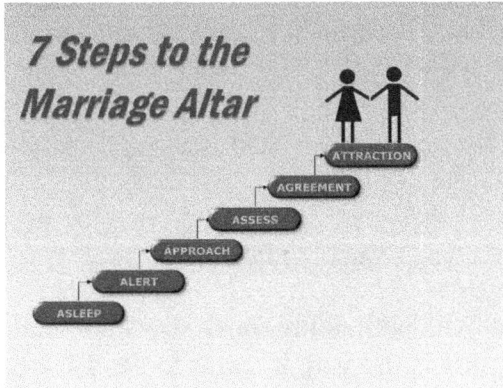

7 Steps to the Marriage Altar

ATTRACTION
AGREEMENT
ASSESS
APPROACH
ALERT
ASLEEP

The sixth step is the Attraction Step. This is the actual betrothal period. Once the agreement has been made, the young man and the young lady are committed to each other and headed to the marriage altar.

I strongly recommend that this period of time not be very long. My suggestion is that it should last no longer than a year, and 6 months is wise. The commitment to marriage has alredy been made. If this period of time stretches out too long, it just causes undo pressures on the couple.

It is during this time that the attraction begins, and the affection is built in the relationship. During this time the young man and the young lady begin spending time together with supervision, talking to one another, getting to know one another better, and learning to care for each other. However, there is no physical involvement yet. You will notice in the picture that they are getting closer, but still not touching or holding hands.

As they share their hearts with each other, their emotions become involved and they begin to love each other. From the point of agreement on is where the romance comes into play. Now the young man begins to woo and to romance his young lady, writing love notes, sending roses, buying her special gifts.

It is also a time of emotional bonding—of getting to know each other and learning to love each other. There is also a security built for the young lady, because she knows that they are committed to marriage.

I have seen young men and young ladies get betrothed before and think, "Will she really love me? Will he really love me? Will we really like each other that much?" But once the decision has been made, the love comes quickly after.

It was that way with both of my sons. Now I am seeing that with my daughter. But that is the way it ought to be. The affection and the security that is built during this time is necessary. The young lady knows that he loves her, he loves only her, and he will always be there for her. What a way to start a relationship!

This is the time to get to know each other, a time of intellectual sharing and heart sharing. What you feel, what you desire, where your heart is at, what you think—these are all things that should be shared during this time.

As you begin to lower the walls you have built around your heart and share with one another and come into a connection with one another, you begin to become one. That is God's intent. This is done by spending time with one another during this period.

It is a time spent with supervision. They are still people with fleshly appetites. For their own safety and protection, there needs to be supervision in order to help them keep hands off.

This is also to be a time of fine-tuning of the young man for the lady. He is learning what she likes, what she doesn't like, what she needs, and how to fine-tune his connection with her. During this period, they are adjusting their likes and dislikes, learning to give and take.

Chapter Eight
Step Seven—the Altar

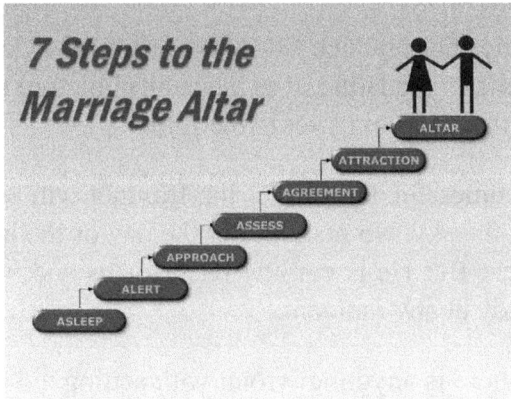

7 Steps to the Marriage Altar

The marriage altar is a period of time set apart for the young man and the young lady to publicly exchange their vows. It is at the marriage altar that the young man claims his bride. What makes a couple husband and wife is the exchanging of the public vows in a culturally and biblically acceptable manner. It is at that point that they become husband and wife.

In our society the time of the wedding is normally set by the young lady and her family. However, in Bible days, it was customary for the young man and his parents to set a window of time during which the wedding was to take place.

That window of time could be a few weeks or a few months, and the young man would determine when during that period of time he would go get his bride. The young lady did not know when he was coming, but she would have her attendants staying at her house during this time, getting ready.

On the day that he had chosen, the young man would get his wedding party together and they would start winding around the streets of the town, playing music. He was going to get his bride.

They would arrive at the door and knock. Then he would call for his bride. The young lady and her attendants would come out, and he would whisk her away to the wedding ceremony.

I am not saying that practice has to be followed today, but that is how it was done in the Bible. It is a beautiful picture of the rapture of the church that is coming yet in the future.

When Jesus comes for His Bride, the trumpet will sound and He will appear in the sky. No man knows the day or the hour when He is coming back. But He is coming back for us and we need to be constantly ready at any moment.

I don't think there is anything wrong with setting a date and a time for the wedding ceremony, and I think all parties need to be involved. There are several things to consider before the date is set.

For the young man, he is getting his house ready, preparing a home for his bride. In the Bible, a young man needed to build a house, and he needed to have enough money set aside to quit work for one year. The Bible puts it this way, "To cheer his wife up." Any lady that has ever gotten married, you know why that needs to happen.

The purpose of all that was so he could connect with his wife. They need to get to know each other without all the pressure of daily life pushing them. Now, I am not saying that we need to do that today, but you should be financially secure enough that the finances aren't going to put pressures on your marriage going forward.

Young man, you need to give attention to getting to know that young lady that you are marrying. You don't belong working two or three jobs or working some job that keeps you out all hours and you can't spend any time with that young lady.

You may need to change jobs so you can invest in her life. If you choose your career over your wife, you have no business getting married. Don't saddle her with a guy who doesn't care.

It is at the marriage altar that the physical side of the marriage begins. The first kiss—the one at the marriage alta—is a special one because the young man and the young lady know that they have kept themselves pure for each other.

Conclusion

I hope and pray that some of these things that we have talked about will be helpful, instructive and practical for you—for both the parents, as well as the young people who are looking for a spouse.

Parents, as you are dealing with your children and helping them walk through this stage of life, remember that God's way is always best. Be diligent about following His principles in helping your young people get to the marriage altar.

For those who are grandparents, you have a responsibility to give encouragement to your grandchildren. May you be wise not to encourage a violating of these Bible principles, but rather to encourage them to practical ways of living out these Bible principles.

God did not give us these principles to hurt us or somehow bind us, but He gave them to us to protect us. That needs to be the focus of our attention. We need to be very careful to follow the principles that God has laid out for us, that the name of Christ would not be hurt.

As I mentioned before, you may do things differently. I am not saying that this is the only way to get to the marriage altar. But however you work out the details, determine to hold fast to the three Bible principles. They are the foundation of this whole process.

We need to honor Christ so in turn our lives can best be a witness for the Savior. It takes a full surrender. These things are wise and simple—but they are not easy because they go against the grain of the world we live in.

As Christians, we need to take a stand for what is right, and encourage our young people who have determined to do things the right way. I pray that we will never speak a discouraging word to them, but rather be a help and an encouragement to them.

We need to strive together to bring up our children in the nurture and admonition of the Lord, so their lives can be far better than our lives were, because we did not follow the principles of God.

www.ingramcontent.com/pod-product-compliance
Lightning Source LLC
Chambersburg PA
CBHW060659030426
42337CB00017B/2694